bloom

Maria Asuncion

BookLeaf
Publishing

India | USA | UK

bloom © 2023 Maria Asuncion

All rights reserved.

No part of this publication may be reproduced, stored in a retrieval system, or transmitted, in any form or by any means, electronic, mechanical, photocopying, recording or otherwise, without the prior written permission of the presenters.

Maria Asuncion asserts the moral right to be identified as author of this work.

Presentation by *BookLeaf Publishing*

Web: www.bookleafpub.com

E-mail: info@bookleafpub.com

ISBN: 9789358736144

First edition 2023

To my best friend in the entire world, Li. How many winter storms have we walked through where we couldn't see through the harsh winds and biting frost, yet we always made it through the other end to bask in the pleasant spring weather?

PREFACE

I first started writing this series of haiku while I was hauled in at home, drenched from head to toe after being caught in a terrific snowstorm during a walk. After I washed myself up and tried to cozy up next to the heater, I realized the winter storm was a jarring reminder that I had spring to look forward to. In the meantime, I had to do my best to persevere through a beautiful but bitter winter. I wasn't alone in this, of course. So many of us have to make it through Toronto winters, when the storms are unpredictable but somehow we could always count on it being difficult.

Though winter is not always pleasant, it certainly is stunning to see, as well as hear. So much freshly fallen snow dampens sound all around, and standing out there as the snowflakes fall, it's otherworldly silent, nearly ethereal.

It's a great contrast to springtime, when the sounds are always present—birds singing and bees buzzing, in particular. But in between these two vastly different seasons, there is a time in nature when we see the rot underground from winter's harsh decay gradually blossom into fascinating flourishes. Think of a flower growing from a seed in the soil to a soaring sprout, reaching for the sun to grace it with its warmth. Think of a frog rousing awake after hibernation, ready to take on the day after a cold slumber. I wanted to capture this transition from winter to spring in this book and allow it to reflect the way that as humans, we too often encounter moments of perish, yet we always come out of it stronger than before. We grow, we learn and we persevere, blooming into our own ways of flourishing.

Before you start reading these haiku, I'd like to hint that I've hidden a few words of when certain haiku take place. I hope you enjoy finding these little hidden words, and I hope you find my haiku helpful in your self-reflection during this time, whichever part of your journey you're in. I'm rooting for you!

wake

I awake to late
winter days; the slow thawing
of stubborn snow banks.

hail

We go through the last
snowstorms. Heavy hail, strong winds.
But we are stronger.

ice

The icy sky cries
harsh hail; the warm wind turns the
hail into soft rain.

fog

Forlorn in fog, frogs
awaken after a rest-
ful winter slumber.

block

A massive, muddy
snowbank blocks me. Stumbling, I
march on anyway.

spring

The first week of spring:
snow still melts, but birds begin
to sing symphonies.

unfurl

Sun's up real early.
Flower petals unfurling.
Feels very freeing.

entwine

I see two trees, and
smile at their entwined branches,
as they share the sun.

hide

Bright days become gray,
as the sun hides away for
now, behind dark clouds.

a little, a lot

Rain pours a little,
then a lot. How do small drops
turn into big storms?

escape

The sun's rays escape
really swiftly, when dark clouds
rain down heavily.

rain

It's funny how rain
might make people gloomy, but
it helps flowers bloom.

storms

So many storms on
so many days. I walk drenched,
smiling for nature.

willow

The willow tree stands
tall, yet its branches reach down
to caress the earth.

contrast

The flowers' soft past-
el colors contrast against
the swirling gray sky.

peek

The gray swirls away,
and the sun peeks out, smiling
at the spring flowers.

mate

Blooming flowers and
buzzing bees. A wondrous ma-
ting anomaly.

rare

Rare cherry blossoms
open up, only for a
beautiful moment.

pink

Pink petals adorn
the path, where we walk, taking
in the scenery.

arrive

Flowers bloom to tell
the sun that spring has arrived,
all thanks to its shine.

brief

Spring is brief but sweet,
bringing in warmth that turns in-
to harsh summer heat.

www.ingramcontent.com/pod-product-compliance
Lightning Source LLC
LaVergne TN
LVHW010533210726

843508LV00020BA/2955